NEVER GIVE A FISH AN UMBRELLA AND OTHER SILLY PRESENTS

BY
MIKE THALER

ILLUSTRATED BY
JERRY SMATH

WHISTLESTOP

Troll

For
Matthew and Tina,
Anna and Mary,
From their Stepauthor
—M.T.

For my nephew,
Matthew John Ritsko
Love, J.S.

There are certain presents you should never give certain pets.

For instance . . .

you should never give a fish . . .
an **umbrella**.

You should never give a chicken . . .
lipstick.

You should never give a sheep . . .
a **sweater**.

Or, a lion . . . a **permanent**.

Or, a snake . . . **sneakers**.

You should never give an ostrich . . .
golf clubs.

A kangaroo . . .
a **pogo stick**.

Or, a centipede . . . **stilts**.

You should never give a porcupine . . .
a **balloon**.

Or a **mask** to a raccoon.

Or, a bass . . . a **bassoon.**

And you should never give an octopus . . .
boxing gloves.

Or, a clam . . . a **kazoo**.

And never give a turtle . . . a **girdle**.

Or, a penguin . . . a **sport coat.**

Or, a leopard . . . a **polka-dot tie**.

And you should never give a polar bear . . .
roller skates.

A rabbit . . . **earmuffs**.

Or, a bat . . . **sunglasses**.

And never ever give a monkey . . .
a **marker**.

An elephant . . . a hanky.

A hippo . . . a **tricycle**.

A peacock . . . a **mirror**.

A giraffe . . . a **turtleneck** sweater.

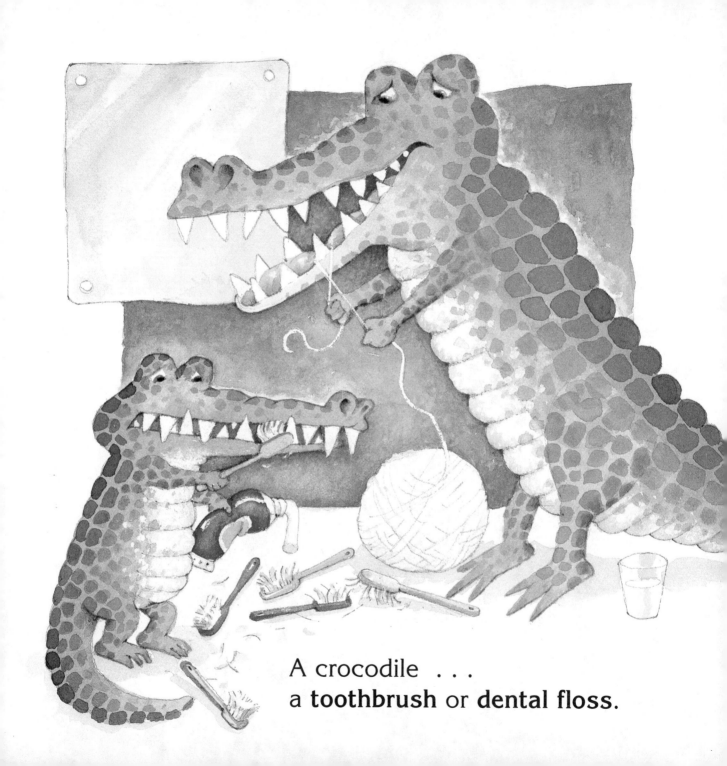

A crocodile . . .
a **toothbrush** or **dental floss**.

A duck . . .
a **baseball cap** and **flippers**.

Or, a pig . . .
silverware and a **bib**.

But don't worry!
You can always give your pet a book . . .

this one!